STEP BY STEP SUMMARY:

WHAT YOU WILL NEED:

- CRAFT KNIFE
- SELF HEALING CUTTING MAT
- WASHI TAPE
- COLORING PAGE

- CHOOSE YOUR COLORING PAGE AND THE ELEMENTS THAT YOU WISH TO USE WASHI TAPE ON.

- CHOOSE A FEW DIFFERENT PATTERNS AND COLORS OF WASHI TAPE THAT WILL COMPLEMENT THE BALANCE OF YOUR COLORED PAGE.

- TEAR OFF OR CUT THE WASHI TAPE TO THE DESIRED LENGTH.

- APPLY THE FOLLOWING STRIPS WITH A SLIGHT OVERLAY TO ENSURE IT STICKS

- PRESS THE WASHI TAPE DOWN ON THE AREA YOU WISH IT TO STICK TO AND TRIM WITH A CRAFT KNIFE TO SIZE

- READJUST ANY STRIPS AS NECESSARY, IT CAN BE LIFTED WITH THE TIP OF YOUR CRAFT KNIFE OR FINGERNAIL

- ADMIRE YOUR CREATIVITY I HOPE YOU ARE INSPIRED TO USE A LITTLE BIT OF WASHI TAPE IN YOUR NEXT COLORING PROJECT.

HAPPY HOUR COLORING

WASHI TAPE IS A COLORFUL CRAFT OR MASKING TAPE THAT HAS MULTIPLE PURPOSES.

BECAUSE IT IS LOW TACK (NOT AS STICKY AS MASKING TAPE) IT'S GREAT TO USE ON COLORING BOOK LIKE THIS ONE.
IT ALSO OFFERS COLORISTS AND CRAFTERS A LOT OF VARIETY.

YOU CAN PURCHASE WASHI TAPE MADE FROM DIFFERENT MEDIUMS LIKE RICE PAPER AND IN DIFFERENT SIZED WIDTHS AND LENGTHS.

THE THING I LOVE THE MOST ABOUT WASHI TAPE IS THAT IT COMES IN SUCH A VARIETY OF COLORS AND PATTERNS.

YOU CAN CHOOSE PLAIN COLORS, STRIPES, DOTS, BUNNIES, WOOD LOOK ALIKE, GLITTER, VELVET JUST TO NAME A FEW.

© 2021 COLORING BOOK HAPPY HOUR

All rights reserved.
No part of this publication may be reproduced, distributed or transmitted in any form or by any means including photocopying, recording or other electronic or mechanical methods without the prior written permission of the publisher, except in the case of brief quotations embodied in critical reviews and certain other non commercial uses permitted by copyright law.

Thank you for your recent purchase.

If you wouldn't mind leaving an online review section, we would really appreciate that. We love hearing everyone thoughts and comments.

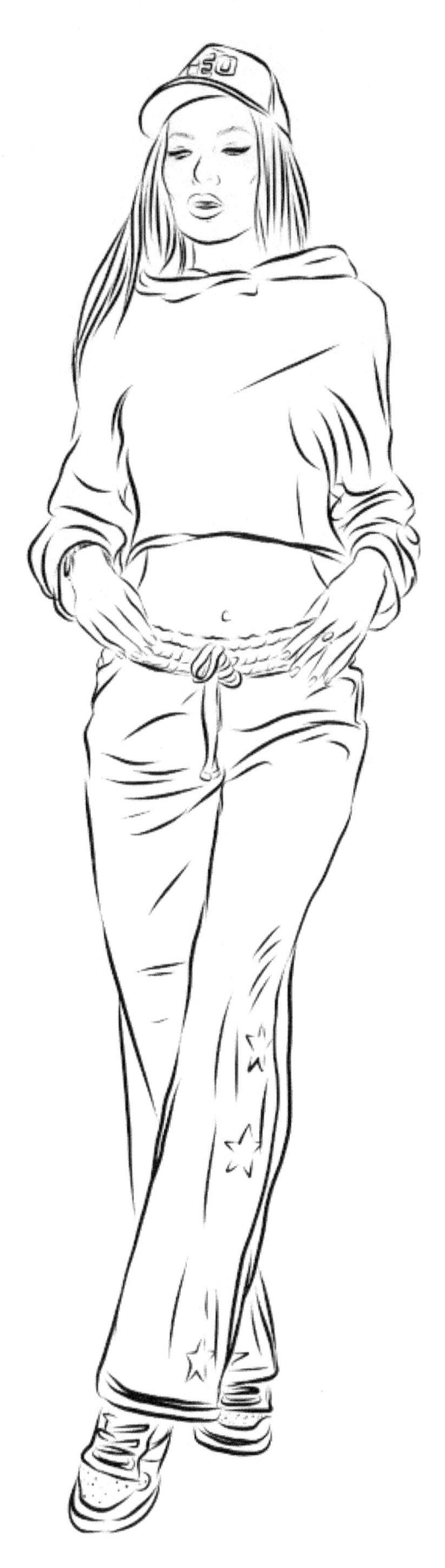

www.ingramcontent.com/pod-product-compliance
Lightning Source LLC
Chambersburg PA
CBHW081156290426
44108CB00018B/2574